Exactly What To Expect As Trustee For Real Estate A Loved One Leaves Behind

Selling the home for the most money, in the timeframe that works best for you, with the least amount of stress

By Kim Ward

Copyright © 2017 By Kim Ward

All rights reserved.

ISBN: 1978215754

ISBN-13: 978-1978215757

DEDICATION

I imagine you are wondering what your next best steps are now that you have become entrusted with the responsibility for your loved one's estate. I offer and dedicate this book to you.

TABLE OF CONTENTS

ACKNOWLEDGEMENTS   i

INTRODUCTION   1

   Preparation for the Transition   2

CHAPTER ONE   6
How to Sell the Home
for the Most Money:
When Opportunity Meets Preparation

   Our Smart Home Selling Process   7
   The Preparation Process   8
   The Home Selling Journey   10
   The 70-30 Rule   11
   The Room-By-Room Review   12
   Through the Eye of the Camera   13
   Pre-Listing Inspection   15
   Clean – Repair – De-clutter – Depersonalize   18
   The Emotional Magic of Soft Staging   19
   Solids for School Pictures and Bedrooms   20
   The Color for Money and Life   23
   It's Showtime – Lights, Lights, and More Lights   23
   A Picture's Worth a Thousand Words   27
   Telling the Home's Story   27
   Making the Home a Box Office Hit   29
   Hitting the Bulls-Eye with Pin-Point Pricing   31

CHAPTER TWO — 35
Timeframe that Works Best for You:
Reasons for Selling

Family	35
Timing	41
Appraisals	42
Buyer Financing	43
Back to Preparation and how it Impacts Timing	44

CHAPTER THREE — 47
Selling with the Least Amount of Stress:
Having a Guide by Your Side to Help Reduce Stress

Investors	47
Personal Property	51
After	56
Real Property and Taxes	57
Having to Respond Quickly	60
Not Knowing	62
Navigating	63
Home Repairs	64
Buyer Home Inspections	65
Title Issues	66
Having Committed to a buyer Who Can't Close	66
What to Disclose	70
The Unknown	71
It's a Wrap	72

CHAPTER FOUR 73
Additional Resources:

10 Questions to Ask Before Choosing a Real 73
Estate Agent

As a Real Estate Advisor, What Do I Do All Day? 76

    Responding 77
    Scheduling Showings and Consultations 78
    Setting and Attending Appointments 79
    Negotiating Offers and Managing the Sale 79
    Problem-Solving 80
    Marketing 81

Raving Fans: What Past Client Have to Share 83

Raving Fans: What Attorneys Have to Share 87

ABOUT THE AUTHOR 90

ACKNOWLEDGMENTS

I want to thank Cyndee Haydon and Charlotte Volsch for being my friends in our Mastermind Group because we get things (including this book) done…together. Thank you Sue Carter, for being my friend and editor, and Ashlie Rivera, my amazing assistant for all your help and patience while writing this book.

INTRODUCTION

I've experienced the loss of my father, a dear friend, and my stepfather George, a wonderful man who loved my mother. All of these deaths have affected me differently. I was 23 when my father passed away. Three weeks prior to his death, I became a new mother. I was unable to really process his passing because I had a child to care for. When my close friend, Emery, passed, I was a young mother of four children. Again, I had a tremendous amount of responsibility and moved quickly, almost robotically, through the tasks that needed to be done to manage his estate. It wasn't until George passed that I was really able to process grief. Being 45 years old, I was more mature, my children were older, and the loss was great. George was more than my stepfather; he was my mentor. Looking back, I'm not sure that he even knew that.

Does having experienced these losses qualify me to help others? Perhaps yes, as my experiences help me to have greater empathy and understanding. And, through the years, I've developed the skills to help others with the details of a loved one's passing so that they may have the space to grieve their loss. Helping others has now become my purpose and it feels like a good way to live my life.

This is a book about what is important when someone is responsible for the real estate that a loved one leaves behind and the truths surrounding such responsibilities. It was written because a client, Dan, the trustee of his sister's estate, asked for it. My first reaction was, "Me? Write a book"? But after thinking about it and how it could help those who find themselves doing something that they never wanted to do, I found my motivation.

I've been helping people with estate properties since 2003. That means I have been involved with hundreds of people, who are experiencing hundreds of different situations and scenarios. And out of all of that, some meager truths have come to the surface to give more insight when carrying the burden of being a trustee and the process of handling a loved one's estate. Sharing my experience as a real estate broker, as well as telling the individual stories of some of the trustees that chose to trust me to help them, is what this book is all about.

Preparation for the Transition

I wrote this book to help you with the emotional shift needed and help you prepare while transitioning to selling your loved one's home. You can feel comfortable because you will know what to expect, how to prepare yourself, prepare the home and ultimately take out much of the stress of this process.

In this book, I focused on the three things that trustees frequently tell me they want:

- to sell the home for the highest price,
- in a timeframe that works best for them,
- and to do it with the least amount of stress

My purpose is for you to be outrageously happy with the help my team and I provide you while we help you understand the necessary steps and are the *guide by your side* through the entire process.

You will find home selling preparation tips and successful strategies to avoid costly challenges and mistakes. You will benefit from the lessons I've learned from being a real estate advisor since 1999 and helping hundreds of trustees. Most importantly I'll share real stories (though the names have been changed to protect their privacy) and real experiences of other trustees, like you, so you may begin the transition of letting go. This includes understanding the journey and the magnitude of what you're about to undertake.

Putting a sign in the front yard and putting the home on the market is the easy part. Choosing the right real estate advisor to personally commit to getting you and your family calmly prepared for and through the process is the unpredictable hard part.

It's often the intangibles that you'll come to value most. Things like communication, patience, responsiveness, accountability, resourcefulness, problem solving, listening and strong people skills that can be hard to quantify. Hearing what others have to say about their experience however, is a good place to start.

So, as you read this book, you may come to better understand the value of hiring an experienced real estate advisor like me with a knowledgeable team. In today's real estate market, it's not just getting an acceptable offer that means success because experience shows, 1 in 5 homes that go under contract never sell! Don't be that one in five.

It's all the hundreds of complexities most people don't know or they assume won't happen to them. It's been shown that it's always in the last 100 feet that you will either be jumping for joy and celebrating success or experience the heartbreaking emotional rollercoaster and financial cost of failure.

One thing is for sure, home selling is an emotional, complex process and money is an emotional topic. Occasionally, I hear sellers focusing on how little they want to pay someone or how they can even do it themselves. This can cause a lot of unnecessary stress. It's better to focus on how to make the most money, with terms and timeline that work for you by choosing a proven *guide by your side*, like me, to guide and get to the celebration of a sold home.

I'm not going to tell you that you get what you pay for because you already know that. Today there are some "low cost looking" models available to sellers and it's often confusing because who wants to pay more than they have to... right?

Real estate advisors, like me and my team, work on a contingent fee. This means we invest all our time, our money and our expertise in getting the home sold. We do all the work, incur all the expenses and only get paid when you are successful. We never just "take listings" because we actually get homes sold and we'll discuss why it's important to understand the difference more inside this book.

As you flip the pages and read, I hope you'll be able to see behind the curtain of the Wizard, and take away some of the mystery of selling. This book gives you a better, deeper understanding of what it takes to sell the home for the most money, with the best terms and the least stress in today's challenging real estate market. You'll discover there are two paths:

- you can decide to take the risky one with little support
- or you can choose the "easy button" working with an expert

When your values are clear, your decisions become easy. May your selling journey be an easy, low stress and successful one!

CHAPTER ONE

How to Sell Your Home for the Most Money:
When Opportunity Meets Preparation

The purpose of this book is to give you a better understanding of the journey of selling the home for the best price with the least stress possible. This chapter will expand on this and give real-life examples, and proven strategies on how to best accomplish this goal. Learning how to prepare a house to sell for top dollar quickly is no easy task, so I applaud you for taking the time to learn more about the process.

The following strategies and insights can be used to help you make better choices with next steps in this process. Let me just say, if you love chaos and drama this book is definitely not for you. However, if you are someone who wants to know how to avoid any added turmoil then continue reading!

Start by asking yourself "What is important about selling this house to me?" You may find it helpful to write your answers. If you have a clear understanding of why you are selling, it will help give you focus throughout the preparation, the marketing and successful sale of the house.

Once you have decided on your reason(s) for selling you can then start working on your timeframe and the Smart Home Selling Process.

Our Smart Home Selling Process:

- Hire a Realtor®
- Room-by-Room Review
- Pre-Listing Inspection
- Cleaning & Repair
- De-Clutter & Depersonalize
- Staging and Photo Preparation
- Soft Staging
- Take Professional Photos
- Pin-Point Pricing
- Coming Soon Marketing
- Full Launch Marketing
- It's Show Time!

The Smart Home Selling Process is a step-by-step guide to getting the home from where it is now, to being prepared, to begin the marketing phase. You, as the trustee, will play a large role in deciding on the timeframe for this process.

Once the home has been de-cluttered and cleaned, your real estate advisor can then begin the marketing stage. The marketing stage includes soft staging, professional photography, and all the advertising that the property is for sale.

Experience shows that the work done in these early steps can result in a 10% or greater increase in what buyers are willing to pay, which is why we address these topics first when we discuss getting the highest price possible. All the negotiation skills in the world won't change a buyer's emotional attachment or desire to want your property. In fact, it is usually the intangibles that move buyers to make their best offer. Many buyers will be educated on the feature, function, benefits and value of the house, but it really comes down to how they feel about the property.

The Preparation Process

- 1) Hire Your Real Estate Advisor
- 2) Room by Room Review
- 3) Pre-Listing Inspection
- 4) Clean, Repair, De-clutter, Depersonalize
- 5) Stage and Prepare For Photos

When we begin to focus on what we need to do to get the highest price, with the most value, leading to the biggest return, we start by thinking about what differentiates the home from the competition. This is an important step, because no one sells in a vacuum.

With all the information available through the click of a mouse, the home can be compared, at any given time, in many different ways with whatever else is available in the current housing market. Anyone can access this information including appraisers, who are part of the buyer's loan process for the purchase of the property. This is why the objective should be to make the house stand out to as many buyers as possible. It is why the Preparation Stage of the Home Selling process is so important.

What we find most often when working with someone selling a home is that it is important to first step back, take off your rose-colored glasses, and take an objective look at the home as it is right now. Then decide what needs to be changed to make it look like what we want it to look like once it is on the market. By that I mean, decide what do you think you need to do to:

- depersonalize and de-clutter?
- identify repairs needed to quickly and easily prepare it for sale?
- or simply have it professionally cleaned?

Once you choose me and my team to help you, we will go into more detail on each of these steps to guide you through the process.

During the Home Selling Preparation, your real estate team goes to work doing all the things that make your home a box office hit. We want it to be the high return investment that you're looking for.

The Home Selling Journey

Now that you've glimpsed at the big picture to start the home selling journey you can see why most people start thinking about, and begin preparing to weeks before they want to sell. Keep in mind that the first, and most important step, is to hire a real estate advisor you trust to guide you through the Home Preparation Process outlined above.

- Staging and Photo Preparation
- Pinpoint Pricing
- Coming Soon Marketing
- Full Launch Marketing
- Show Time!

Completing the Home Preparation Process means that everything you need to do to get ready to move into the marketing phase of home selling is complete. This is why it is so important to have a skilled professional real estate *guide by your side* from the very beginning.

Real estate advisors, like me, who do this every day can also be invaluable in letting you know what repairs and improvements to make and, just as important, what won't provide a good return when selling. Most sellers are surprised to know that many of the most impactful things cost very little money. Let's take a closer look at the various steps in the marketing process.

The 70- 30 Rule

Most people living in a house have 70% of their items decorating and filling space in the home. That leaves 30% actually showcasing the desirable features of the house. It is totally natural to surround yourself with all the things you love. But when selling a home much less personal property will actually showcase the home's features. We want to highlight the strengths of the house that will attract buyers.

This is our focus in the Home Selling Preparation phase – you are transforming space in the home that is filled with what the decedent loved, and bringing the focus back to what we're marketing - the house.

To defend the equity and get the highest offers from potential buyers we need to reduce or remove the personal belongings. By reducing your personal items to 30%, space is then opened up to welcome real homebuyers in the market to imagine their belongings and their family in the home.

This proven process consistently helps our clients make the home more appealing to more potential buyers. Doing these steps up front can not only make more money, it also reduces stress by selling the home faster and proactively removing issues rather than waiting until after a willing buyer has viewed the home.

The Room-By-Room Review

To start the process of reducing the personal items to 30% take notice of the things that are unique and specific to the decedent, such as hobbies, and collections. I've worked with many people whose loved one had a vibrant personality, and the home reflected that vibrant personality. When placing a house on the market it is best to go with subtle and neutral features over vibrant ones. Choosing neutrals will attract the most buyers because it allows each person to see themselves and their belonging working in the space. That is the goal, to allow each buyer to fall in love with a house by seeing themselves living there.

To simplify the process, we have developed a plan known as the Room-by-Room Review. This plan prevents overwhelm and analysis paralysis by dividing the home into sections allowing you, as seller to have a specific plan and to minimize your stress.

In the next section of the book we have included a series of before and after photos of our Room-By-Room results, that way you can see the impact that small, orchestrated changes can make.

There are three parts to the Room-By-Room Review:

- viewing through the eye of the camera
- pre-listing inspection peace of mind
- the emotional magic of soft staging

We make time to go through the home with you, inside and out. We look at each room and what is currently in it. Then we look at how to make the rooms stand out from the competition. You decide as we go through – are you going to:

1. allow family members and friends take cherished items?
2. give away?
3. throw away?

Doing this for each room opens up the space, allowing us to stage, and to create the desired effect we want in each room.

Through the Eye of the Camera

To reduce the overwhelm of preparing the home for sale, we go room-by-room together. In the first part of our Room-By-Room Review we're considering an eye on how we can create more of a blank canvas, and definitely a neutral canvas to be able to tell the story of your house. When we're finished, you have a working plan enabling you to address one space at a time. You see the impact of what you're doing to enhance the features of the home. To get the plan in place we will discover the unintended distractions the camera will pick up and then consider what we want the buyers to focus on in each room.

We know that when we get the home ready for market, it will be online through photos and the camera will not edit it. I've discovered that even when I am coming into a home, often my mind will edit unintentionally. It's really important that we get a good sense of things that may be drawing in people's attention. We can then determine if what draws someone's attention is the focal point that we really want.

This is a simple tip you could do right now. Go to a room you think looks great and take a photo. See if the room looks as great in the photo or if you find yourself looking at something on the floor or something on a nightstand versus seeing the whole room. This is why we always take photos as we're going through the room-by-room review. We are looking at it with an eye toward what we should move to another location or remove completely.

Pre-Listing Inspection

Next, we are looking for what needs to be fixed or repaired. All of these things are really an important part of our ability to defend the equity and ultimately get the best price. Why? Because every little repair, every little flaw in a buyer's mind triggers their natural inclination to exaggerate the repair costs. Some research has found that buyers assume the cost to fix something is much more than it actually turns out to be and they want compensation for it. It's always better to fix what can be fixed cost-effectively, up front. Every little detail we can take care of before opening the front door for homebuyers is going to make for a much smoother process throughout the transaction.

This is why we do a Pre-Listing Home Inspection. Even the most conscientious homeowner will have things that need to be fixed. It's so much better to find out now and take care of cost-effective. We may not discover everything because we won't be crawling into the attic or under the house, but we will look at the interior and exterior of the home together. Experience shows that it really helps increase buyer interest.

We will next determine what items you want to fix and what you want fixed by a handyman. Another benefit is that taking care of these things up front can be done more cost effectively because you are choosing the plumbing fixtures, lighting, flooring, etc. Once you're under a purchase agreement, the buyers may request all work be done be a licensed professional which I don't have to tell you will always cost more.

Example Repair List - 123 Main Street

Preliminary Staging

- Pack all personal photos
- Living room-move white table from entry into corner of living room
- Remove rug
- Remove all stuffed animals and minimize pet toys
- Kitchen-remove magnets from refrigerator and minimize items on the counters
- TV room-move sofa under window, pack and store personal property
- Office-pack unused items and tidy up desk areas
- Patio- remove cover from table and chair set

REPAIRS/TO-DO

Exterior of home

- Hose down or power wash exterior including fascia board and eaves
- Wash and spray paint security screen door
- Replace white motion light at exterior of garage
- Replace damaged ceiling fan in garage with a white light

Example Repair List – 123 Main Street (cont.)…

- Paint front and north side fencing (dark brown)
- Install dark brown mulch in planter beds
- Continue to water front yard
- Install outlet cover at west side of garage
- Paint cover at rear patio by electrical panel (white)
- Replace vertical blinds at sliding door in living room

Interior of home

- Paint exterior of front door (blue)
- Caulk master bathroom shower
- Clean track of sliding glass door so that it slides easier

Items to Purchase

- White exterior light for garage
- White interior light to replace damaged ceiling fan (garage)
- Ceiling fan (master bedroom)
- Two globe light (master bathroom)
- Mulch for planter beds
- Exterior cover for electrical outlet
- Vertical blinds for living room sliding door

Schedule handyman that we recommended to help with repairs

Schedule professional cleaning company that we recommended

Clean – Repair – De-clutter – Depersonalize

Now that we have completed the Pre-Listing Inspection and the Room-By-Room Review you will have a specifically crafted plan on what to do to prepare the house for the market. We can also help you with a list of trusted vendors who specialize in everything from deep cleaning to home repairs. We can even provide you with a referral to individuals who specialize in de-cluttering and depersonalizing the house. That way if the task is too much for you, you will have the help you need versus the hard task of doing the work alone.

This is a time when I like to remind my sellers that when we do everything right you can expect to sell the home quickly usually in less than 45 days. It's worth the preparation and it will be less hectic for you once you're under contract for the sale.

I won't to go into much detail because each home gets a very specific preparation plan. I will share that if you only choose one thing to get your home ready it should be white glove clean. Most buyers believe clean equals well maintained, and not clean equals not maintained. If the home is not clean, experience shows that buyers will immediately start looking for the homes weaknesses. My experienced recommendation is do whatever it takes to clean up thoroughly. This includes the most overlooked items when preparing a house for sale and that is the windows, so take the time or allow one of my vendors to detail them. Remember, because we work with professional photographers they will be shooting through the windows to bring the outdoors in and those windows must sparkle!

As far as repairs, we will work with you to determine what must be done based on your specific situation, what makes financial sense to take care of, and what to disclose and let the next owner determine how to handle.

The Emotional Magic of Soft Staging

The third, and final part of the Room-By-Room review is creating an emotional attraction to the house. This is what all potential buyers are looking for; to feel the excitement of *this is home.* To help visually attract homebuyers, my team has been trained to use a technique called soft staging. The best way to explain soft staging is taking what is available in the home (or what we have stored in our staging warehouse) and creating vignettes that sell the lifestyle potential buyers are wishing to lead. Buying is an emotional process. What my team and I do as our seller's trusted real estate advisors, is bring that emotional and magnetic attraction to each room, so buyers "feel at home".

The home can subliminally become more attractive to buyers with just a few strategically placed items. This is why we suggest you team with a real estate advisor that is a marketing expert rather than your average real estate agent. When you hire a marketing expert, like me, before we ever place the house on the market we are at work using proven strategies to market it to sell quickly and just as important to sell for top dollar.

A picture is worth a thousand words and I've created a few examples so you can see how the Room-By-Room Review can make your house more visually attractive to potential buyers.

Solids for School Pictures and Bedrooms

Do you remember when you were a kid and your parents prepared you for picture day at school? Or when you ever had a family photograph? What's the first thing a photographer tells you when preparing for these events? To wear solid colors! Why? Because solids will "stand out" in the photo better then prints and patterns. As the subject of a photograph we look best when we wear solid color, and the same is true for each room in your house.

A lot of times homeowners will have bedspreads with patterns and prints and it's distracting and sometimes can distract buyers. A dynamic change can happen in a room when you take a neutral colored bedspread that is complimentary with the room paint color. It can be a very inexpensive purchase that will highlight the room and make it stand out. It is just like when you see your childhood school picture and you're wearing that solid shirt, you show well, and that is the same for well-staged rooms.

When selling the home, it becomes a house and it is no longer about what you like. You are presenting the house as a product and in the master bedroom the goal is to make it feel like a relaxing retreat. Need a visual?...just imagine a 5-star hotel room and if you're not sure, Google any of the major hotel chains. Hilton, Holiday Inn, etc. and you can check out their room photos online. Those nice hotel rooms have solid colored bedspreads that look clean and crisp. In our own homes our bedspreads can be comfy and we love them because they're comfortable but probably a bit worn. But this can cause your buyer to subliminally equate worn with dirty. If some of the furnishings can stay in the home, including the master bedroom set, my team will provide updated, neutral bedding. Buyers are looking to buy a "new home" with a "fresh start"; presenting the home as crisp and clean is always a winner. We are creating the effect of walking into a hotel room; that "ahhhh, I can relax here, this is my sanctuary, this is tranquil, and inviting." It's a simple tip that has a huge impact when the camera is marrying the look of the room to the emotion created in the potential buyer.

Master Bedroom Before

Master Bedroom After

The Color for Money and Life

Another important tip you cannot underestimate is the power of having something green or simulated living in several rooms of the house. If you don't have a green thumb, you can simply use artificial plants. When artificial plants don't fit you, it could be as simple as a green vase or some other item that's green. Since we've de-cluttered and created that blank canvas, now we have to make sure that the environment doesn't feel sterile. A simple green silk plant or some fresh flowers add a lot on photography day. Now that I've shared this tip with you, the next time you're in a staged home, at department stores or other decorated places you'll likely notice that there's always something green.

Some other elements from nature are seashells or twine balls that people may notice and subliminally connect as living items. Knowing how to use these subtle vignettes and strategically positioning inexpensive accessories are not the kind of things the average real estate agent may have studied and mastered. From knowing how to show a vibrant room in photos to creating the space that feels alive when buyers walk into it is what my team and I can do for you.

It's Showtime – Lights, Lights, and More Lights

The final soft staging tip is to check all the light bulbs. We make sure that we have the highest wattage light bulbs in all the lighting. All lights should be plugged in and working.

Living Room Before

Living Room After

Buyers are naturally attracted to brightness; if you've watched any home tv shows you always hear the compliment of "the home is light and airy." We want to create the feeling of sunlight because people tend to feel happier when there is light. If the home has any rooms that are dark because of the angle of the sun or because of trees, we will really let the wattage of the light bulbs work for the house. We are basically bringing the outdoors in and creating that really bright feeling.

Occasionally sellers will say to me, "This is so bright and it's brighter than I'm used to," yes, it is, and think of it just like when you go to the theater. On the stage those lights are bright because we want to see the actors; we're creating that same effect. When we do everything right, the homes are in demand and sell quickly. Remember this is the house's show time and we are creating the atmosphere to let it shine!

Estate representatives have shared that they were outrageously happy with our preparation because we are differentiating their loved one's home so that it looks great and looks better than the competition.

One of the things that surprises my clients is they often think they're simply hiring someone with a real estate license. Over time they come to appreciate that what makes the difference in their experience is that choosing an advisor who is a really strong marketer and negotiator begins with preparation. That's why we spend whatever time it takes to prepare the house before we take the next steps.

Dining Room Before

Dining Room After

A Picture's Worth a Thousand Words

I often use my cell phone camera to capture the before photos during a Room-By-Room Review. These photos are just for the beginning and I would never market the estate's biggest asset using those photos. We have professional photographers and we work together to capture what I like to call the "money shots". I know what they are in each house and I make sure my photographer gets them. As we're going through the house, I already know who are the most likely buyers. As we go through the home, we consider the different examples: will it be someone that is probably going to have a growing family, or is it somebody that is looking to retire here, or is it an investment? We then make sure we're highlighting those features visually to them.

Telling the Home's Story

Now we are ready to skillfully craft the story. Each house has a story that we're sharing with the next owner. Our job is to couple the story with our knowledge of the market and consider what buyers want, what they are looking for, and how to best convey that to them.

We've talked about how it all starts with the soft staging, then the photography, and it moves into the marketing arena.

Kitchen Before

Kitchen After

We then apply our market knowledge, and do the pinpoint pricing. We look at:
- how does this house compare?
- what are its strengths?
- how do we minimize any weaknesses?
- how to best compete?

We differentiate between the potential buyer objections, which we can handle, and the property condition, which we cannot change, but can minimize. As a last resort, you must be prepared to mitigate with price.

For example, if you have a house that is on a busy street or backs up to a highway and its noise, there's nothing that can be done to change that. But, because of our marketing knowledge, we know how to price appropriately and focus on the positives. We market each house appropriately to attract the person who is going to appreciate the positive features versus someone who won't.

Making the Home a Box Office Hit

We've already learned that what's most important for home sellers is that they have an expert marketer and negotiator that just happens to have a real estate license! When you have this combination, you have someone who is looking at everything through an experienced and unique lens.

Game Room Before

Family Room After

Let's put the emphasis on how my team and I can professionally present this home as a box office hit. We focus on our plan for the grand opening with the red carpet rolled out that is going to be so attractive that many buyers are going to be lined up to see it first. That's what can happen because you're choosing a team who knows what potential buyers want and know what's going to capture them.

We are building the scene, writing the script, setting the stage, making sure everyone looks their best with primping and make-up and then the director captures it all on film. When it's all done the teasers come out to let people know it's coming soon, to build up the excitement and then the big day is here. The red carpet is rolled out and since we've done everything right, you experience big financial results, fast. When it comes to the house, the goal is multiple offers quickly; especially when we're in a strong seller's market.

Hitting the Bulls-Eye with Pinpoint Pricing

We can start working early on with you to prepare; however, we won't know a pinpoint price until we know when you're ready to put it on the market. We know some people will need a few months, some people will take three or four weeks, and some less than a week. Each property will require a different timetable to get it all done, we are going to discuss the timeframe that works best for you in the next chapter in much more detail.

As you get closer to being ready and the home being available for buyers to purchase, just know the market is ever changing. It's dynamic like the ocean. It ebbs and flows. To get specific we need to know when you want to go to market.

When you're ready, then we take all that information and we can build a plan to say "here's right where the home is and here's right where the market is going to receive it well".

So when you're ready to put the blockbuster of a home "on the market" – it's time to review the "price of admission". We start by reviewing all the information that impacts what the highest price is at any given time. We look closely at the current competition, we look at what's pending a sale (currently under contract), and what's sold in the last 180 days and we build our case for buyers and appraisers, too, so they see the value! We discuss and decide how to adjust for any items that you decided not to fix. We talk about what conditions exist that can't be changed and will ultimately impact the price; for example, the home being in an industrial area, having a messy neighbor creating a bad view or in an airport flight path.

We take all this information and with all our experience help sellers zero in on a real pinpoint price of where the market is when they are actually ready to hit the market.

People pay more for things they perceive are a good value, desirable and special – it's that "It Factor" and we all know "it" when we see "it". We've been making the buyers feel that way about the home through the whole preparation process (where we decided to give it away or throw it away and taking care of needed repairs), as well as, differentiation from the competition by using emotional vignettes, using soft staging, positioning, photos, marketing, pinpoint pricing and more.

You can hopefully understand now why the Preparation stage is so important as well as the Marketing stage – these give the biggest return for the least expense!

All of this chapter is about getting the home on the market; however, it's my strong negotiating skills that ensure that the buyers and the appraiser see the value so that you end up at closing with every dollar you deserve. To end up with the most money possible, you really need to find an expert marketer and negotiator with a real estate license who has the time and attention to dedicate to your success. I am that person!

CHAPTER TWO

Timeframe that Works Best for You:
Reasons for Selling

Family

Expanding somewhat on the point of family, I'd like to share a little bit about some of the relative issues or concerns my clients have encountered. As you can imagine and could be experiencing right now, family is a very big piece of managing the whole estate process; hence, there are many potentially sensitive obstacles of which to be mindful. When family members and friends have an emotional attachment to the person who is gone, I've witnessed the good and the not-so-good. I've seen family members get along wonderfully with each other; working together to take care of all the tasks that need to be addressed to settle the estate. I've also witnessed the flipside, when the trustee is doing their best to manage an unhappy or uncooperative family member.

The difficulty is usually the result of some kind of a family dynamic or because a family member has some issue and will not respect the trustee's position of authority. Although having been put into the position of representing the estate, some family member or members can make life more difficult. This makes moving through this process challenging. And, not surprisingly, problems frequently involve the decedent's personal property. Sometimes a beneficiary believes that the decedent told them that they could have certain possessions but nothing was written down.

> *When Scott's brother passed away, his nephew, Dennis, was the only beneficiary. Both Scott and Dennis thought that once the house sold, they would receive the proceeds from the sale quickly. It did not take them long to discover that was not exactly the case. As Dennis had been living in the home and was in dire need of funds to pay for a new place to live, the attorney was able to engineer permission to advance some funds from the decedent's other assets.*
>
> *Scott received the emergency funds and Dennis was able to obtain housing. Most of the remaining proceeds from the estate, including the sale of the house, were disbursed to Scott in the following weeks. The good news for Dennis was that his father had additional assets to accommodate the emergency funds request.*

To protect themselves and the estate, the trustee may be in a position of having to make hard choices. Having a will is helpful because the trustee simply follows the decedent's wishes as written in the will. When there is not a will, the assets, including the real estate proceeds, are distributed as directed in the trust. Regardless of whatever conversations may have occurred between the decedent and family members or friends, the trustee will determine the division of the assets. But explaining the process to the beneficiaries can be a challenge for the trustee. The good news is that most of the time, when beneficiaries understand the process because it has been adequately explained to them, they are cooperative. While the trustee is executing these responsibilities, it really helps to be connected to a skilled estate attorney.

Because the trustee is experiencing their own mourning and emotions, even while dealing with the other beneficiaries (who may be mostly family), keeping the two roles separated can be challenging. Having an attorney as part of your team gives you someone to field questions to and perhaps step in to help with the sometimes more extreme issues, also known as the "messy stuff."

What a relief it can be to have the attorney come along and represent what is to be done according to the law, protecting both the trustee and the estate. Additionally, when it comes to situations where family members are doing things outside of what needs to be done, your attorney can take action to get things back on track. In some cases, the attorney can relieve you by actually having those conversations with the family, including the family member that is not cooperating.

The unattached person, the attorney, can be what one of my clients referred to as "the bad guy." The attorney is someone to metaphorically stand behind you and say, "Well, nevertheless, this is how it has to be." And the trustee can then simply continue with the things that need to be addressed with less tension and uncomfortable feelings.

> *Vincent's Uncle Randy passed away, leaving Vincent responsible as trustee of his estate. The trust read that the personal property and home were to be sold and the proceeds shared with Vincent and his three siblings.*
>
> *Vincent's brother, Ralph, lived a few miles from their Uncle's home. When the family met to talk about the disposition of the estate, Ralph shared that Uncle Randy had promised that he could have the house and pay the remaining beneficiaries $1,000 per month.*
>
> *Because Uncle Randy had left a trust with specific instructions, Ralph quickly realized that although he believed he was entitled to the home, his Uncle's wishes as written in the trust must be adhered to. Ultimately the three siblings equally shared their Uncle's gift of proceeds from the home.*

One last thought I want to touch on is how to keep things as calm as possible by keeping the beneficiaries informed. If the beneficiaries don't know the steps that are being taken, they might get anxious. They may start talking amongst themselves and because they don't have a clear picture, may begin to imagine things that aren't really happening.

In most cases keeping the beneficiaries informed does not have to be in the form of any official paperwork, it can just be conversations with them. Communication always alleviates stress for people no matter what process they're going through. When the real estate advisor has a system to keep the trustee informed, then the trustee can pass accurate information to the beneficiaries. When people know what to expect and they know what is happening, experience shows that the process goes much smoother.

Because I just mentioned the real estate advisor as part of the whole process, I'd like to share a bit about the necessity of having a skilled, experienced real estate advisor. This should be a person, like me, who has the right skills, the right experience and knows how to help you with the many details associated with the decedent's home.

It's never too early to partner with a real estate advisor who is an expert at helping trustees with the decedent's home. The largest asset is typically the home of the decedent, including the personal property, and it proves to be the most time-consuming part of representing the estate.

Having a professional orchestrator of the real estate process I imagine would be a relief for several reasons. I use the words "professional orchestrator" because my help is very much about orchestrating. My purpose is to provide the answers to your questions, to present your options, to introduce you to people that can help with the personal property, and to guide you through the preparation, marketing and successful sale of the decedent's home.

Others like you have shared their relief of having someone, like me, to help them make decisions and move forward swiftly.

Another benefit is that the beneficiaries begin to feel comfortable because they see that steps are being taken and appreciate the progress. As your real estate advisor,

> *Laura moved into the family home a few weeks prior to her Mother's passing. Her sister, Elaine, was appointed as trustee of the estate. Everything seemed to be moving in the right direction until Elaine and her brother, Steve, realized that Laura had no intention of cooperating with the distribution of personal items and the sale of the home. They knew that something needed to be done because the home had a mortgage on it and they were having to pay the monthly payment that Laura refused to pay.*
>
> *After several months, Elaine's attorney recommended that she hire a fiduciary to take over her responsibilities as trustee. The fiduciary quickly realized that Laura would need to be forcibly removed from the home and began the proceedings by hiring a legal group that specialized in evictions. The legal process was followed and eventually Laura was removed from the property by the sheriff. The locks were changed and a temporary alarm system was installed Elaine was relieved that, shortly thereafter, the home went on the market. Within a few weeks, multiple offers were received, negotiated, and the home was sold.*

at a minimum, you will receive a weekly update that can then be shared with the beneficiaries. This can be accomplished by including important information about the decedent's home with current facts that can be forwarded easily. Again, I work to help you and the beneficiaries to feel calm, and trust that everything is going well.

Timing

When you decide to sell the home, the first thing you must consider is what is your timeframe… the timing that works best for you. Timing will drive everything else. From there we can help you build a strategic, specific action plan to make it happen.

Timing means different things to different people. I see the range from, "I want to sell immediately, how quickly can we get it on the market and sold?" to "I'm sort of in the three to six month's timeframe."

Regardless of whether it's something that you've been thinking about for the last few weeks or have thought about, talked about, mulled over for few months, you'll appreciate sitting down for an hour with an experienced *guide by your side* to help prepare you for the journey.

What I've noticed is when it's an immediate life experience that makes it necessary to move quickly, it's a relief to know that someone is going to help take care of all the details. These are the details that you may not know about or simply don't have time for because you still have your full life.

For example, if someone passes away and you're responsible for their estate, you still have your life and your family to take care of. It could be that the property is in another city or state from where you live, and there are many details that must be addressed. Often there is a need for immediate relief to have this all handled. Other trustees, like you, have shared that knowing they have the help needed to make all the decisions and orchestrate those decisions, is priceless. To get it all done while going on with your life and keeping you informed of the process, allows you to feel comfortable and meet the timeframes that are required by the estate.

When timing requires you to move quickly, having experienced professionals, your attorney and your real estate advisor, handling details while you are elsewhere, can be a relief. When I am your real estate advisor, you can be where you physically need to be while critical details are being handled. This includes all the frequent and necessary communication to you every step of the way.

Appraisals

Most buyers need to get a loan. When a lender is determining the buyer's ability to repay the loan, they are also making absolutely sure that the amount they loan plus the buyer's down payment equal the current value of the property.

It's important to know that appraisals are an art, not a science, and the most significant variable is what similar properties have sold for within the past six months. Appraisers prefer properties within 1/2 mile of the subject property, within up to 20% of the size and then they make adjustments from there. An appraiser rarely knows if the price of a comparable home was lower because the person living there had to sell because of a life changing issue like divorce, death or relocation.

As an advocate for our sellers, we make sure to educate appraisers on the "backstory" of comparable homes, as well as, all recent improvements, so that our seller's homes get the highest possible valuation. Appraisers are busy people and because in most cases we know the neighborhood better than they do, it's worth the effort to compile this data for them. It assures a much better result for our seller. A side note is that because I meet the appraiser in person at my client's homes, I have not had a bad appraisal in over ten years.

Buyer Financing

What you may or may not know when you're on the selling side, is that while the buyer has submitted an earnest money deposit, much of the time they have a financing contingency in the contract. What that means, to you, is that the buyer can still have a glitch with financing and this contingency allows them to cancel the contract, and get all their earnest money back.

Most sellers have plans and look forward to the completion of the sale. Much of the time there are carrying costs for the property, ie. mortgage, taxes, insurance, utilities, etc. There are times when the only asset is the home and the cost of these items falls onto the trustee. The trustee will be reimbursed after the sale, but until the sale is complete, the trustee carries the financial burden. These financial implications are why it's so very important to have a *guide by your side* to help make decisions that minimize the risk and costly mistakes that trustees can experience.

Back to Preparation and how it Impacts Timing

When considering timing, what we can help you understand is realistically what can get accomplished in what time frame. Sometimes this means while you might be perfectly capable of doing things yourself, to help shorten the time frame and the burden, you may choose to outsource tasks to someone else and enable us to get to market quicker.

Many improvements go a long way to defending equity and it's important to consider *cost effective repairs* for the home. The proposed time frame will determine what gets done, how things get done, and we can help with prioritizing. We can also help by introducing trusted vendors to you because sometimes it's less stressful to have someone else do some repairs and preparation.

We take care of our selling families throughout the transaction process because selling a home can be one of the most stressful things one does in life, especially with the addition of mourning the loss of a loved one.

So how do we minimize stress?

The timing is often like a pressure cooker so we get organized and make sure that things don't explode. We know how to get you through the process in a calm, organized way, and get help when you need it.

> *Jason and Camille, wanted to sell their home in La Mesa. Their decorating style was already very updated, neutral and appealing to most buyers. To help the buyers imagine themselves living there, I helped Jason and Camille to depersonalize. There was a list of things that needed to be repaired and they asked for an introduction to a handyman. Once the repairs and a bit of painting were done I helped with minor, yet buyer emotionally impactful staging. I loaned them a new bedspread and made sure we had something green in every room. I recommended they move an entry table to a different location in the living room. We needed enough time to get professional photos, as well as time to prepare their customized marketing plan so that everything was ready when we came to the market with the maximum exposure. The good news is from the time they chose to sell to having the home on the market, was just 10 days!*

Having a skilled, experienced, and focused *guide by your side* who can lay out some different options around timing is critical. I will help you determine the time it would take for you to do it yourself, including material cost, and then weighing that out against the estimate of someone else doing the work. That way you can determine how much of your valuable time you want to take versus paying someone else, and whether you want to do that trade off, or not. You'll have concrete comparisons so you can make that best choice. It's all about what's most important to you while you are selling the property. It's my job to give you two or three good options that you can choose from, and then you can decide what would be best for you and your specific situation. The good news is that you can rely on me as your go-to person, *your guide by your side.*

CHAPTER THREE

Selling with the Least Amount of Stress:
Having a Guide by Your Side Helps to Reduce Stress

In this chapter we cover selling with the least amount of stress while dealing with highly complex situations. I've mentioned selling the home can be one of the most stressful events in life. Most of the stress is created because of dealing with unknowns. Having a good communicator as your guide is critical. It's important that you understand the market, the pricing, and the preparation. My team and I keep you updated and informed every step through the selling process because experience shows, that's important for reducing your stress. The selling process is very time sensitive, and with frequent updates you will be able to respond quickly. This ensures you don't miss any opportunities to defend and protect the price of the home, literally defending your equity.

Investors

When I speak with a trustee, they often share that they have been approached by investors via phone calls and letters. The investors are offering a quick fix for the sale of the estate property (see Examples 1 and 2).

Kim Ward

Dear ▓▓▓▓

My name is ▓▓▓▓▓▓▓ and I would like to take a moment to offer my condolences on the passing of ▓▓▓▓▓▓▓▓. While I know this can be an emotionally sensitive period, you may also be facing some serious decisions with which I may be able to assist you.

Per public records we've been made aware that you've been named as the Personal Representative for the estate of ▓▓▓▓▓▓▓▓.

Often times, real estate must be sold in order to pay taxes and other outstanding obligations. We purchase real estate and other personal property found in estates. It is our understanding that the property located at ▓▓▓▓▓▓▓, San Diego, CA may be available to purchase. If it is, we are interested in making an offer. We would like to purchase the property; we are not real estate agents who simply want to list it.

While we do not know your particular situation, we are prepared to do what is best for you and the estate. We buy real estate, both residential and commercial, paying all CASH and with a quick closing. We purchase properties in their "as-is" condition, avoiding the costly time of needed repairs to qualify the property for financing. We also purchase real estate contracts, notes, mortgages, and other types of accounts receivable, automobiles, furniture, jewelry, or anything you need cash for.

Please keep in mind that you do not have to wait until the probate process is completed to sell anything. As the Personal Representative for the estate, the courts have given you the authority to sell the property.

Please call me at ▓▓▓▓▓▓▓ today to discuss how we may be able help you in further detail. I look forward to speaking and working with you.

Respectfully,

I'm so sorry for your loss ♡ Please let me know if you need help with anything.

Example 1 - Letter from investor

September 16, 2016

Dear ▓

First, let me take a moment to offer my condolences on the passing of your loved one, ▓▓▓▓▓▓▓▓. While this can be an emotionally sensitive period, you may also be facing some serious decisions with which I may be able to help.

I'm writing about the property located at: ▓▓▓▓▓▓▓ San Diego, CA ▓▓▓▓. Often real estate property must be sold in order to pay taxes, pay any outstanding liabilities and to pay the legitimate heirs. I buy real estate found in estates and would be interested in making an offer.

Selling this property is probably not a priority for your family. If in the future the heirs decide to sell, please call and I'll be happy to make an offer.

Some of the advantages I may be able to offer are: (1) I can buy the property in its "As Is" condition. (2) You needn't do any fix up or clean up. (3) I will pay all cash. (4) I can close the sale very quickly, often thirty days or less and (5) You can save the 6% charged by most real estate agents.

If you decide to sell the property, I can simplify the process. Once I've looked at the property I'll figure the net cash price to offer you. I'll budget for a basic remodel (to bring the property to top condition) and a small margin for surprises. If you'd like I'll make a written proposal to you. Once we agree on price then we open escrow.

I hope you understand that you do not have to wait until the probate is completed to sell the property. As the Personal Representative of the estate you have authority (under the Independent Administration of Estates Act) to act on behalf of the estate, cash out the asset and proceed to final distribution.

If you're interested give me a call at ▓▓▓▓▓▓. I wish you all the best.

Yours truly,

▓▓▓▓▓▓

Example 2 - Letter from investor

These investors are trying to convince the trustee that they are the best option for an easy sale of the home, with promises of short escrows, no real estate commissions, and no extra fees. As the trustee you may think, easy equals done! However, these investors have not seen the interior of the house, and most of the time, have not even driven by the property. Hence they do not know the condition of the property, and are just looking to buy at the lowest price possible.

Experience shows that once the investor has viewed the property, including the interior, they will often make claims about the property such as, "Oh. I didn't know that it needed a new kitchen and bathrooms." This is the point where they will negotiate tens of thousands of dollars less than their initial offer.

The bottom line is that investors are representing themselves; they are not representing the estate. This means that anyway they can find to decrease their initial price is a win for them and a huge loss for the estate.

Investors will sometimes offer no extra fees, a misleading deal to say the least; with all the price-cutting, they can easily afford to absorb any additional costs such as paying the estate closing costs. The investor's goal is to entice the trustee to take their offer before they wise up and find an experienced real estate advisor to represent them and the estate.

To prevent investors from taking advantage, the trustee should meet with a real estate advisor, like me, who can give them the honest facts about the property's value. As a real estate professional, I am not trying to buy the property; my purpose is to represent you and the estate, as well as, to negotiate the highest price possible, with the best terms. There is a saying: "Negotiating for yourself is like preforming surgery on yourself, and you would never do that now, would you?"

The trustee may have concerns that the cost of a real estate professional's commission will cut into the extra funds for the estate. However, experience shows this is not the case because the negotiated price so greatly exceeds the price offered by an investor that it more than covers any commissions. The trustee's job is to maximize the amount of money for the estate. Experience shows selling to an investor, without representation, will surely decrease that net proceeds for the estate.

Personal Property

Although the biggest asset of most estates is the real property…the house, there is more property to consider. The belongings of the decedent are part of the personal property, including furniture, cars, appliances, clothing, jewelry, etc. What should the trustee do with these items? First the trustee should partner with their attorney and determine if the beneficiaries will be allowed to remove mementos from the property. Beneficiaries often want items of value inventoried to be included with the total estate value. However, sometimes there are valuable items that the family members wish to keep and, it is up to the trustee to determine what may be removed from the estate. During this step, the trustee should try their best to be considerate as there are often items the beneficiaries wish to keep for sentimental reasons.

Once the family members have removed all desired mementos, the remaining property will need to be liquidated. It is important to keep in mind that the personal property may not be worth anything near the amount it was originally purchased for. The trustee has three options for liquidating the estate: have an estate sale; sell the entire estate to a buyout company; or donate the remaining items. An estate sale is worth the effort if the estate has a large number of valuable items remaining that can be sold individually by an estate liquidator. Estate sales require a six-to-eight-week period for marketing and planning; if there is enough time available, this may be a good choice for the estate. Once the estate sale is finished, all the remaining items will need to be removed, sold to a buyout company, or donated.

The second option the trustee may choose is to sell to a buyout company. The company hired to do the buyout will assess all the personal property and then give a price they will pay to remove everything. Buyouts are convenient because they will remove all the items, including the items that are not saleable. Once a price has been agreed upon, the buyout company will schedule a date to clear everything out, usually less than a week later. This will give the trustee an empty property to put on the market, quickly.

The third option is to donate. When choosing to donate items, anything that is small needs to be boxed up prior to having it picked up by the donation company. Someone has to box up all of the items, either the trustee, family members, or someone from the outside who is hired to do so. A list needs to be made of the items that will be donated and submitted to the donation entity so that they will know how much room they need on their truck. The donation company is then scheduled to come in and remove everything. Like a buyout, this option provides the trustee with a completely empty property fast, which means getting the house on the market sooner.

Whichever method the trustee chooses to pursue, keeping thorough records of what items are removed at what time is important. The trustee should try their best to protect themselves with good record keeping. For more detailed information regarding the three options for managing the decedents personal property, either visit www.ProbateAndTrustHelp.com/free-real-estate-ebooks/ or, if you prefer we can send you a copy, just call my office at 619-741-0111.

The trustee can rest easy if they have an experienced real estate professional help them handle the personal property of the estate. Many times, the trustee does not live where the house is located and they need a trusted real estate advisor, *a guide by their side,* like my team and me, to be their eyes and ears.

Having a skilled real estate professional coordinate how to take care of the personal property will keep you, the trustee from feeling overwhelmed, especially if you live out of state.

Kim Ward

Kim Ward, REALTOR®
Call Today: (619) 741-0111
CalBRE #01218310

HORIZON REAL ESTATE
PROBATE AND TRUST HELP

Personal Property Dos, Don'ts and Options

Marie traveled 1,700 miles because she was appointed as the trustee of her mother's estate. When she arrived, her first scheduled task was to secure the home and all of her mother's personal property. The next day her brother and sister met with her at their childhood home. They began the process of going through all the memories and choosing things that were important to them. They soon became overwhelmed with the thought of what was to happen to all the things that they couldn't take to their own homes and turned to me for guidance.

After talking about the three options - Estate Sale, Buyout, and Donation - the family decided to have me schedule with the buyout company to give them a bid for removing all the things that they left in the home. Because Marie anticipated it would be a lot of physical work, as well as an emotional toll, Marie was relieved that she did not have to pack up all of the things that were left.

She agreed to the buyout bid and an appointment was scheduled for the removal. Because she needed to go home, she gave me permission to give access to the home to the buyout team. Once the remaining personal property was removed, I took photos and emailed them to Marie. She was happy that the next step would be to prepare the home for sale; the home was officially on the market a week later.

> *Rosalia was named trustee of her friend's estate and became responsible for two properties in San Diego and a third over 600 miles away in Truckee.*
>
> *The largest property located in the North Park area of San Diego had been her friend's home; it also had a second house that had tenants living in it and provided rental income. At our Initial consultation, we weighed the benefits of repairs and updates vs selling as-is. Rosalia chose to increase the net profit for the estate by improving the property. Spending just over $5,000 on cost-effective repairs, including painting most of the interior, hardwood floor repairs, power washing the front porch, and a few miscellaneous items proved to be the right decision.*
>
> *At the neighborhood open house, many compliments were received. The neighbors that had been in the home prior to the decedent's passing couldn't believe the transformation and even asked me for the name of the paint colors! And, the best news is that the home sold for 99% of the list price, which made the beneficiaries very happy with Rosalia.*

After

When the personal property has been addressed through one of the three options and the preparation, the marketing, the negotiating, and all the many details of the real estate sale have been completed, the net proceeds from the real estate sale can be wired directly into the estate account.

It's important for you to know that, in addition to orchestrating the steps through the sale of the property in the estate, I am also here for you as a lifetime resource. Feel comfortable reaching out to me with any questions you may have around the estate, as well as for any real estate situation outside of the estate. Always think of me as your go-to resource when you or someone you know has questions and want accurate answers.

Real Property and Taxes

The real property, the home, is usually the biggest asset of an estate. Before it is sold and before the beneficiaries receive their portion of the proceeds, there are some issues that a trustee needs to consider regarding taxes and the estate.

A question that I'm frequently asked by the trustee is, "Is there anything I need to know regarding taxes and the estate?" Because tax laws are changing all the time, I always ask the trustee if they have a tax professional. A tax professional will know the current tax laws and can answer any tax associated questions for the trustee. If the trustee does not have a tax professional, I recommend contacting an attorney for a referral to someone that can answer inquiries concerning the proceeds and potential tax liability. As a wise advisor, I know I can't be all things, all the time. However, as the orchestrator, I often give introductions to other key players. This has proven to be quite stress reducing for the trustee.

The trustee should never use personal banking accounts for handling any financial assets of the estate as it can create questions from the beneficiaries about how the trustee is using the estate funds. To help achieve this, the trustee can obtain a tax ID number (EIN) for the estate by going to https://www.irs-ein-tax-id.com

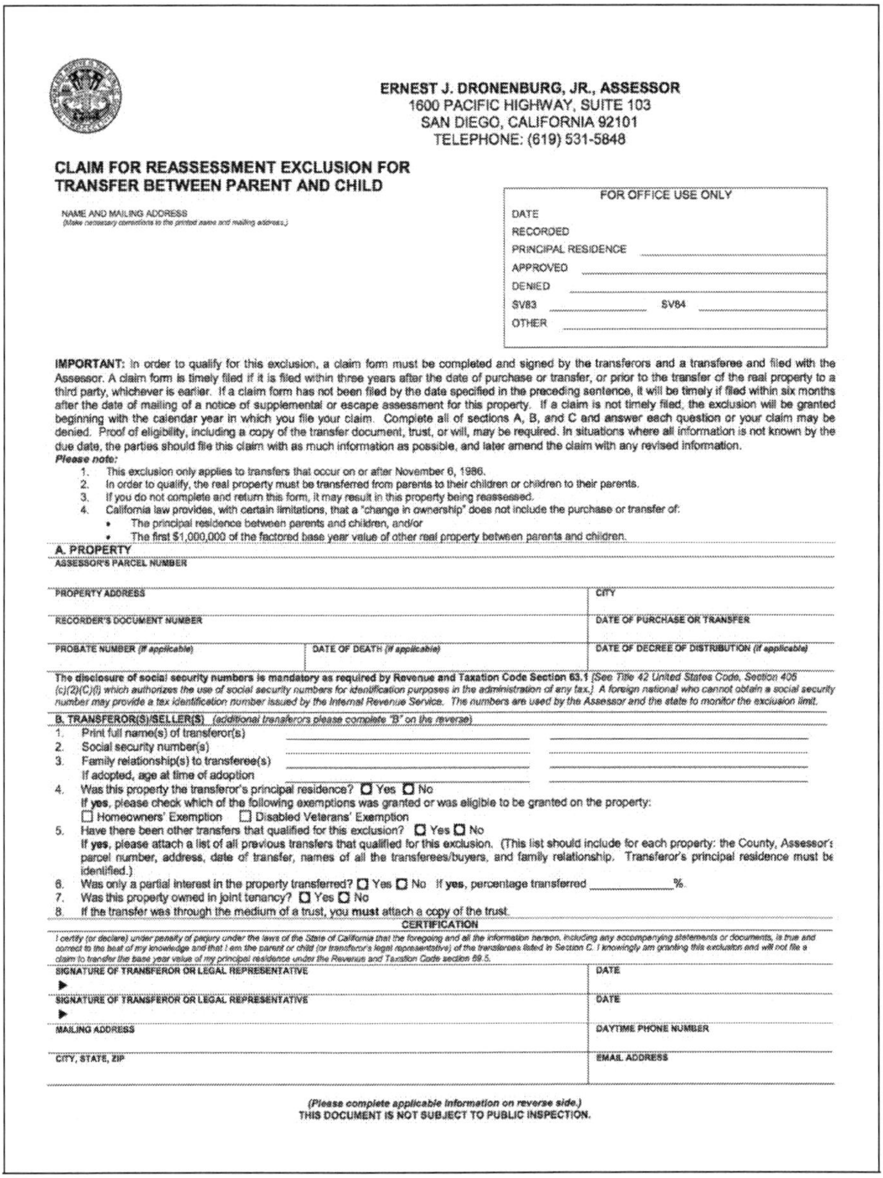

ERNEST J. DRONENBURG, JR., ASSESSOR
1600 PACIFIC HIGHWAY, SUITE 103
SAN DIEGO, CALIFORNIA 92101
TELEPHONE: (619) 531-5848

CLAIM FOR REASSESSMENT EXCLUSION FOR TRANSFER BETWEEN PARENT AND CHILD

NAME AND MAILING ADDRESS
(Make necessary corrections to the printed name and mailing address.)

FOR OFFICE USE ONLY
DATE
RECORDED
PRINCIPAL RESIDENCE
APPROVED
DENIED
SV83 SV84
OTHER

IMPORTANT: In order to qualify for this exclusion, a claim form must be completed and signed by the transferors and a transferee and filed with the Assessor. A claim form is timely filed if it is filed within three years after the date of purchase or transfer, or prior to the transfer of the real property to a third party, whichever is earlier. If a claim form has not been filed by the date specified in the preceding sentence, it will be timely if filed within six months after the date of mailing of a notice of supplemental or escape assessment for this property. If a claim is not timely filed, the exclusion will be granted beginning with the calendar year in which you file your claim. Complete all of sections A, B, and C and answer each question or your claim may be denied. Proof of eligibility, including a copy of the transfer document, trust, or will, may be required. In situations where all information is not known by the due date, the parties should file this claim with as much information as possible, and later amend the claim with any revised information.

Please note:

1. This exclusion only applies to transfers that occur on or after November 6, 1986.
2. In order to qualify, the real property must be transferred from parents to their children or children to their parents.
3. If you do not complete and return this form, it may result in this property being reassessed.
4. California law provides, with certain limitations, that a "change in ownership" does not include the purchase or transfer of:
   - The principal residence between parents and children, and/or
   - The first $1,000,000 of the factored base year value of other real property between parents and children.

A. PROPERTY

ASSESSOR'S PARCEL NUMBER

PROPERTY ADDRESS | CITY

RECORDER'S DOCUMENT NUMBER | DATE OF PURCHASE OR TRANSFER

PROBATE NUMBER *(If applicable)* | DATE OF DEATH *(If applicable)* | DATE OF DECREE OF DISTRIBUTION *(If applicable)*

The disclosure of social security numbers is mandatory as required by Revenue and Taxation Code Section 63.1 *[See Title 42 United States Code, Section 405 (c)(2)(C)(i) which authorizes the use of social security numbers for identification purposes in the administration of any tax.] A foreign national who cannot obtain a social security number may provide a tax identification number issued by the Internal Revenue Service. The numbers are used by the Assessor and the state to monitor the exclusion limit.*

B. TRANSFEROR(S)/SELLER(S) *(additional transferors please complete "B" on the reverse)*

1. Print full name(s) of transferor(s)
2. Social security number(s)
3. Family relationship(s) to transferee(s)
   If adopted, age at time of adoption
4. Was this property the transferor's principal residence? ☐ Yes ☐ No
   If **yes**, please check which of the following exemptions was granted or was eligible to be granted on the property:
   ☐ Homeowners' Exemption ☐ Disabled Veterans' Exemption
5. Have there been other transfers that qualified for this exclusion? ☐ Yes ☐ No
   If **yes**, please attach a list of all previous transfers that qualified for this exclusion. (This list should include for each property: the County, Assessor's parcel number, address, date of transfer, names of all the transferees/buyers, and family relationship. Transferor's principal residence must be identified.)
6. Was only a partial interest in the property transferred? ☐ Yes ☐ No If **yes**, percentage transferred ______%.
7. Was this property owned in joint tenancy? ☐ Yes ☐ No
8. If the transfer was through the medium of a trust, you **must** attach a copy of the trust.

CERTIFICATION

I certify (or declare) under penalty of perjury under the laws of the State of California that the foregoing and all the information hereon, including any accompanying statements or documents, is true and correct to the best of my knowledge and that I am the parent or child (or transferor's legal representative) of the transferees listed in Section C. I knowingly am granting this exclusion and will not file a claim to transfer the base year value of my principal residence under the Revenue and Taxation Code section 69.5.

SIGNATURE OF TRANSFEROR OR LEGAL REPRESENTATIVE ▶ | DATE

SIGNATURE OF TRANSFEROR OR LEGAL REPRESENTATIVE ▶ | DATE

MAILING ADDRESS | DAYTIME PHONE NUMBER

CITY, STATE, ZIP | EMAIL ADDRESS

(Please complete applicable information on reverse side.)
THIS DOCUMENT IS NOT SUBJECT TO PUBLIC INSPECTION.

Figure 3: Dronenburg, Ernest J., Jr. "Claim for Reassessment Exclusion for Transfer Between Parent and Child." (n.d): 2-3. 14 May 2016. Web 30 Nov. 2016. <https://arcc.sdcounty.ca.gov/Documents /58AHPCEXCL.pdf>

C. TRANSFEREE(S)/BUYER(S) *(additional transferees please complete "C" below)*

1. Print full name(s) of transferee(s) ____________________ ____________________

2. Family relationship(s) to transferor(s) ____________________ ____________________

If adopted, age at time of adoption ____________________

If stepparent/stepchild relationship is involved, was parent still married or in a registered domestic partnership *(registered means registered with the California Secretary of State)* with stepparent on the date of purchase or transfer? ☐ Yes ☐ No

If **no**, was the marriage or registered domestic partnership terminated by: ☐ Death ☐ Divorce/Termination of partnership

If terminated by death, had the surviving stepparent remarried or entered into a registered domestic partnership as of the date of purchase or transfer? ☐ Yes ☐ No

If in-law relationship is involved, was the son-in-law or daughter-in-law still married or in a registered domestic partnership with the daughter or son on the date of purchase or transfer? ☐ Yes ☐ No

If **no**, was marriage or registered domestic partnership terminated by: ☐ Death ☐ Divorce/Termination of partnership

If terminated by death, had the surviving son-in-law or daughter-in-law remarried or entered into a registered domestic partnership as of the date of purchase or transfer? ☐ Yes ☐ No

3. ALLOCATION OF EXCLUSION (If the full cash value of the real property transferred exceeds the one million dollar value exclusion, the transferee must specify on an attachment to this claim the amount and allocation of the exclusion that is being sought.)

CERTIFICATION

I certify (or declare) under penalty of perjury under the laws of the State of California that the foregoing and all information hereon, including any accompanying statements or documents, is true and correct to the best of my knowledge and that I am the parent or child (or transferee's legal representative) of the transferors listed in Section B; and that all of the transferees are eligible transferees within the meaning of section 63.1 of the Revenue and Taxation Code.

SIGNATURE OF TRANSFEREE OR LEGAL REPRESENTATIVE	DATE
SIGNATURE OF TRANSFEREE OR LEGAL REPRESENTATIVE	DATE
MAILING ADDRESS	DAYTIME PHONE NUMBER
CITY, STATE, ZIP	EMAIL ADDRESS

NOTE: The Assessor may contact you for additional information.

B. ADDITIONAL TRANSFEROR(S)/SELLER(S) *(continued)*

NAME	SOCIAL SECURITY NUMBER	SIGNATURE	RELATIONSHIP

C. ADDITIONAL TRANSFEREE(S)/BUYER(S) *(continued)*

NAME	RELATIONSHIP

NOTE: Effective January 1, 2009, Revenue and Taxation Code Section 63.1(j) allows a county board of supervisors to authorize a one-time processing fee of not more than $175 to recover costs incurred by the county assessor due to the failure of an eligible transferee to file a claim for the parent-child change in ownership exclusion after two written requests have been sent to an eligible transferee by the county assessor.

THIS DOCUMENT IS NOT SUBJECT TO PUBLIC INSPECTION.

Figure 3: Dronenburg, Ernest J., Jr. "Claim for Reassessment Exclusion for Transfer Between Parent and Child." (n.d): 2-3. 14 May 2016. Web 30 Nov. 2016. <https://arcc.sdcounty.ca.gov/Documents /58AHPCEXCL.pdf>

With this new tax ID number, bank accounts can be opened to handle any use of funds related to the estate, including the funds from the sale of the decedent's home.

Another important point in regards to taxes is property taxes. Upon the decedent's passing, the San Diego county tax assessor will reassess the property tax to represent their determination of the current market value of the house.

If all of the beneficiaries happen to be children of the decedent, there is a special document called the Parent-Child Exclusion document (see Figure 3). This document can save the estate thousands of dollars, but it is frequently overlooked.

How will it save money for the estate? Often the home was purchased many years earlier. When the decedent purchased the property, they were locked into a lower rate of property tax based on what they paid for the house. Upon their passing, the San Diego tax assessor's office reassesses the property taxes based on the current market value. In many cases, this assessment can mean an increase of hundreds of dollars per month to the property expenses. It often takes six months to a year from the date of death to the date the property closes escrow, which can equate into thousands of dollars in potential savings for the estate if the original tax rate can be kept.

Having to Respond Quickly

Technology is one of the best ways to really span those geographical distances. Having the ability to respond quickly relieves the stress when an offer is received, especially in timely markets. Whether it's a buyers' or sellers' market,

> *At our initial consultation to discuss the steps to prepare, market and sell his mother's house, Bob was surprised to learn that the San Diego county tax assessor's office would be adjusting the yearly property taxes from the amount his mother had been paying. The county assessor's office reassesses the taxes based on what they determine to be the market value of the property. Bob learned that as of his mom's date of death, the property taxes would increase substantially, from $1,027 per year to $6,060, based on a current property value of $485,000. I'll do the math for you: that's an increase is $5,033 annually, a whopping $419 per month. In this case, if the home were sold six months after his mother passing, the estate would pay $2,516 to the San Diego county tax assessor Now for the good news. Because Bob chose to have me help him prepare, market, and sell his mother's home, he was pleased to learn about the parent-child exclusion.*
>
> *In this case, because the children of the decedent (Bob and his siblings) were the beneficiaries of the estate, property taxes do not need to increase. I helped Bob to fill out a Parent-Child Exclusion document and submit it to the San Diego assessor's office. This kept the taxes at the amount his mother had been paying, saving the estate thousands of dollars.*

people are looking for quick responses so that they can move on with the next steps. The ability to get that information in front of you, the seller, whether you live locally or in another area by using technology is critical. Often trustees are employed, and may not have the time to communicate about the preparation, the marketing and the efforts taking place regarding the sale of the home every day. By using technology, the smart advisor gets the information to the trustee so they can reply with all their questions. This type of communication helps ensure that the timeline required to respond to the buyer isn't missed. In the case where there are co-trustees, everyone is getting the same data and accurate answers to the questions, so that everyone is well-informed of the next steps.

Not Knowing

Our human mind immediately goes to negative or guarded thoughts when we are in situations of not knowing. For example, if you come home today expecting your son or daughter to be there and they aren't, we usually don't think, "oh, I'll bet they stopped to give a friend a ride home after school and they'll be here any minute." We usually are thinking some horrific thing has happened and an uneasy anxious feeling comes over us.

As we help people with selling a home, one of the biggest financial choice of their lives, we are very sensitive to the need for them to be communicated with regularly. The communication includes what is happening now and what is happening next, to eliminate the stress of "not knowing".

To make communicating complete, it is imperative that your advisor really listens to what is being said and how you are saying it. That way the responses are appropriate to your need. You may need help right now, or someone to listen, or be searching for a solution and reassurance. All of those different things come into play at different times. Experience shows that when you have a *guide by your side* who is competently handling the unknowns and communicating what they are doing, you feel confident, and this brings relief. My team and I have got you covered in this journey with the biggest financial choice of your life.

Navigating

This brings us to navigating through the entire process. Having professionals on the trustee's team, dealing with the family, the timing, the taxes, the investors, and the personal property, can be exhausting! The first thing is securing and maintaining the property. That can include getting all the utilities transferred into the trustee's name, rekeying the property, and possibly having a temporary alarm system installed. As your real estate professional, I can help with all of these details and more, achieving the ultimate outcome of protecting the property.

An important step to maintaining the home is to make sure that the property insurance is kept up to date. Sometimes the decedent's insurance company becomes aware that the home is vacant and cancel the property insurance. When that happens, press the "easy button" and simply ask me for a referral to a company that will provide vacant house insurance.

The next step with almost every home to prepare it for viewing by homebuyers is to consider repairs, and then hire a cleaning company. As your real estate professional I may recommend cost effective repairs, provide an approximate expense for the repairs, and when you agree, help get accurate bids from vendors. The plan would be to have the repairs bring the property up to a point where traditional buyers, rather than an investors, want to submit an offer.

Traditional buyers ultimately pay much more than an investor, which is why these repairs may be the best step. For example, having the property professionally cleaned will cost between $200-$450 and ultimately make a great impression for traditional homebuyers. Every home is unique. Whether the property is a fixer and the best scenario is to simply sell as-is, or it is determined that, with a few cost-effective repairs (fresh paint, updated lighting or new flooring) can earn thousands of dollars more; you can feel comfortable that I will help you with these choices.

Home Repairs

The National Association of Realtors or NAR says the average person moves every twelve years. Getting a home ready including finishing needed repairs can be overwhelming because frequently people don't know who to trust, and what repairs will give the best return. Then there is the scheduling and supervising the work to be done. We can help to reduce your stress of repairs because of our experienced and organized team. We have trusted plumbers, an electrician, handyman, several painters, a landscaper, a tree trimmer, etc. Helping you press "the easy button" is our promise and goal.

Trustees have shared that the hardest part is not really the expense for the preparation of the home for sale, the hard part is knowing who to trust to do the work, and getting on their schedule. We've found that because we have worked with the vendors previously, and established a good working relationship, our clients often become the vendors' priority. When we tell the plumber, the handyman, the landscaper that we need the work completed in a timely fashion, they honor that.

> *Diane recently called me to tell me she had tried to call three electricians to get a quote and no one would even return her call. The electrician that we gave her not only returned the call, but showed up when they said they would. The electrician asked Diane to send pictures ahead of time so they could be fully prepared. They showed up on time, did the work and Diane called me to say "wow! what a difference in treatment, and thank you for the introduction."*

Buyer Home Inspections

The decedent may have lived in the home a long time. Some trustees are surprised that some things aren't in working order. Much of the time the decedent may have forgotten it doesn't work because "it's always been that way".

When buyers make their offer, they are expecting a well-maintained home. The buyer's home inspection is when in a matter of hours, the buyer's love affair with the home goes from engagement to wedding plans, or they get worried.

That's when having an experienced real estate advisor, once again, becomes critical. Remaining calm and respectful when having conversations to discuss concerns is an art. Having the ability to negotiate a win-win to address what has been discovered is a skill. This is when you need someone, like me, to oversee the details because you want to avoid the home going back on the market and everyone wondering "what's wrong with this house?"

Title Issues

It's very important to have the title search completed before going on the market. Issues are frequently discovered and most trustees are completely unaware of existing title issues. Most of these title issues simply require time to have them corrected. We don't want to discover something that may take three weeks to correct once we have negotiated a purchase agreement. When we find a problem ahead of time, we have the opportunity to get it cleared up.

Having Committed to a Buyer Who Can't Close

A buyer who can't close poses incredibly large ramifications to the sale and will be stressful for the trustee who hasn't considered this possibility ahead of time. Sellers often don't understand the problems until they're in a situation where there are no options. A common nightmare situation is a buyer who can't get the loan a week before closing the transaction because they didn't have a preapproval with a solid lender. I always speak with the lender to make certain the lender has researched the buyer's credit, verified income and employment, plus provided proof of funds needed for down payment and closing costs. I do this so that we all understand the depth of the prequalification.

Once we have negotiated with a buyer, we have a timeline for inspection, appraisal and removal of all contingencies. What this means, to you, is that I am overseeing everything to be absolutely certain the buyer and their agent are working towards removing all contingencies. Experience shows 95% of the time, once all the buyer's contingencies are removed, the transaction closes escrow. I am able to oversee everything that is happening because my team has a system with checkpoints. These checkpoints are to the trustee's advantage to be certain the transaction is progressing according to the purchase contract, while protecting the trustee so they don't experience costly consequences.

There's nothing that creates stress like big financial surprises. All the work of getting the home ready for the market, and to have the rug pulled out from under you at the last minute is just emotionally devastating. Our goal is to make it look easy and feel stress free. That is mastery, many years of experience, and systems, plus great teamwork, that makes it feel easy, which is what we strive for.

It's really that last hundred feet that makes or breaks it all, and that is where the biggest financial consequences come in. Being left with a vacant house, and possibly still making mortgage payments because something goes awry can cause double the stress level. Many trustees have limited funds left by the decedent, and don't personally have thousands and thousands of dollars sitting there to fill a gap to maintain the expenses for the house in case there's a "whoops".

Those last hundred feet are when the big whoops can happen, sometimes causing one or two extra mortgage payments. When a delay happens, you'll have extra fees for the utilities, insurance and taxes. There are a lot of moving parts in those last hundred feet. If you don't have the right person managing those moving parts, things get dropped and it's expensive.

> *Recently we were referred to Michael, a trustee from Denver who was responsible for his father's estate. Because it was a sellers' market we knew with our preparation and marketing the home we would be under contract quickly.*
>
> *The first weekend we had over 20 showings and received multiple offers. The first offer received was full price. Michael was ready to sign; however, I encouraged him to wait until I could speak with the buyer's lender. I knew what he didn't; that 1 in 5 offers accepted doesn't close and often it's because of financing glitches.*
>
> *I always want my clients to feel comfortable, but I knew it would be better if he had one restless night rather than to accept the offer. Especially because there were so many other buyers interested in the home; I asked him to trust me. I wanted to make sure he didn't make a decision that got him stuck in a contract for up to thirty days only to be more stressed and disappointed if the buyers were unable to qualify for a loan. He agreed to wait, and when I called the lender the next morning I learned that that the buyers were self-employed.*

> *While they were doing great with their businesses, the hurdle was that if the lender used the normal two tax returns filed, their loan wouldn't be approved. I also learned this mortgage broker was changing companies in two weeks, which is why the buyers had requested 45 days for the loan commitment and close of escrow. These are the type of hurdles that can be addressed early on, when the right questions are asked.*
>
> *Because I do this every day I knew to ask more questions and get a better idea of the risk involved. When I spoke with Michael the next morning, he shared that he hadn't slept well. He said the stress of not having a buyer under contract for the home was much harder on him than he ever thought it would be. I shared what I had learned with him and that we had another offer, a better offer, and that while I hated to have him lose a night's sleep being so worried, I was happy he wasn't going to be disappointed later. Michael was very thankful that I was protecting the estate's financial interests.*

It's similar to asking the professional plumber to come in and repair the problem because the owners tried to do it themselves and created a flood. The plumber came in and used his special screwdriver and it was fixed. They say, "$150? you were here for only 15 minutes and you turned the screw that much." The plumber says, "I knew which screw to turn and how far to turn it, and we see what happened when you didn't."

Realize that as a seller you have a lot of control before you choose a real estate professional, and also again when accepting an offer. Once you accept a buyer's offer you can be stuck with little or no options until the buyer doesn't perform. You have a lot more risk financially and a lot more potential for emotional stress.

What to Disclose

Helping people understand the seller disclosure forms can alleviate a lot of stress. Some trustees might consider putting minimal information down on the forms. It's important to take the time to go step-by-step answering all the questions and checking the boxes that apply. If you're uncertain, then simply ask your real estate advisor. I can help you to understand the purpose of each question on every document. By doing a thorough job, you not only fulfill the requirements, but you protect yourself and the estate from future issues.

No matter the condition of the home and its defects, the right thing to do is to accurately complete the documentation, and provide the information to the buyer when they are excited about becoming a homeowner. It's the surprises after becoming a new homeowner that make the buyer have buyer's remorse.

Helping you with disclosing everything you know about the home is another way that we relieve stress during the process because it keeps you feeling comfortable, and moving the transaction forward in a methodical, calm, and planned manner.

> ## DID YOU KNOW?
>
> State Law requires a seller of a property to disclose to the buyer all known facts that materially affect the value of the property being sold and that are not readily observable or known to the buyer. The seller disclosure forms are designed to help you comply with the law. As trustee, you will have minimal disclosures, but, it is still prudent to address everything you know about the home…in writing.
>
> This is the link to learn more about seller required disclosures:

The Unknown

When I am facing something unknown it's important to me that I know there is safety and security, that way I can feel comfortable. With all things that are unknown to us, things that we need take care of, get done that's where having a *guide by our side* is necessary. It is critical having a skilled professional who can react to what is and come up with creative solutions so that we continue moving forward. This is the opposite of going, "Oh no!!!", creating drama or wasting time complaining about what happened. A guide can actually step up and say "this is what happened, this is how we can resolve it…are you good with that?" or "here are two other choices, which would you prefer?" Meanwhile they are continuing in that forward progress.

It's a Wrap

It's not unusual to want the treasure!
It's the prize at the end of the rainbow ...
It's the big *hooray* at end of the race ...
It's the box office hit at the end of the red carpet ...

And the preparation...the practice, the sweating, the falling down, the bandaging up bruised knees and ankles, the ice packs, the late-night planning for a new angle, the glitch in technology that prevents or delays a step, the needed doctor visit that delays time and eats into costs...all this is not what we want.

We all can relate to this part because somewhere we've experienced setbacks. When our eye is on the prize we want to catapult over the setbacks straight to victory.

This time you can...

Reach out and "press the easy button" and call 619-741-0111. My experienced team and I will help you get from where you are to where you want to be with ease and grace.

CHAPTER FOUR

Additional Resources:
Ten Questions to Ask Before Choosing a Real Estate Agent

If you're thinking about selling a home, one of the first things you'll need is an experienced real estate agent. Chances are you may already know one from within your own social circle or have received referrals from neighbors, friends, and family members. For those of you starting from scratch, online tools are also available and can provide extensive background to help you find your perfect match.

No matter how you decide to search for your agent, you'll need to know what to ask them before you begin your journey together. You are going to be spending a lot of time with your agent so his or her style had better be compatible with yours. Do you need someone easygoing or someone aggressive? I imagine you like working with someone similar to yourself. You may want to work with someone with an easygoing personality, a great sense of humor or perhaps someone who is assertive. What is most important because you will be working with them over the next few months, is that you feel comfortable with that person.

Here are ten questions that you could ask your potential real estate agent or broker before you hire them to help you with the preparation, marketing and sale of your home:

- What percentage of your clients are sellers vs. buyers?

- How many estates did you represent in the past 12 months?
- Will I be working with you directly or handed off to anyone else other than you? In other words, will you handle all aspects of my transaction or will you delegate some tasks to a sales associate or administrative assistant? (A knowledgeable assistant can be invaluable to an agent, but you, the seller, want to make sure you can connect with your agent regularly.)
- Do you work full-time or part-time as a real estate agent?
- How many homes have you closed in the past year?
- How many other sellers are you representing now? How many buyers? (Hint: the busiest agents often are the most efficient.)
- Is your license in good standing? (Check an agent's certification yourself with your state's Department of Real Estate. Many states provide this information online. For example, in California residents may check at www.dre.ca.gov and click on Verify a Real Estate License.)
- How many years of education and experience do you have? (Experience and continuing education typically make for better agents.)
- Are you also a broker and/or a Realtor or simply an agent?
- Can you provide me with the names and phone numbers of past clients who have agreed to be references? (Insights from past customers can help you learn more about an agent and give you a greater comfort level.)

If the agents check off this list then you're on the right track. Use this list to compare agents. But one word of caution is this: Do not pick someone so close to you that you can't have a serious "straight talk" business conversation. You need someone with whom you are comfortable asking any question and sharing all your concerns. And keep in mind that this person will at some point become quite intimate with your entire financial picture.

Choose the most qualified person for the job that you think you'll work well with. The ideal person for you is:

- an experienced professional
- who knows your market
- acts in an ethical manner
- answers all of your questions
- addresses your concerns and
- most important, will listen to you and be your teammate throughout the entire process.

As a Real Estate Advisor, What Do I Do All Day?

It certainly is not as easy as it looks on TV. As a real estate advisor, my job is to manage all the people involved in a transaction, making sure that they do their job. I must quickly adapt to what needs to be done to keep the transaction moving forward and also respond in a timely manner to client needs.

So where to start? Explaining how I spend my time is like attempting to explain what a doctor or lawyer does all day. There's a lot more that goes into "treating patients" or "handling legal matters" and the same goes for my life of helping people prepare, market and successfully sell property.

From a consumer's first thought about making a real estate move to actually taking the leap (whether that means right now, next month or a year from now), as your advisor, I am incubator, initiator, action-taker, coordinator, scheduler, personal concierge, resource person, problem-solver, mediator, miracle worker (sort-of), red-tape cutter, transaction manager and chief make-it-happen officer.

These are the general categories:

- Responding
- Scheduling showings and consultations
- Making contact
- Setting and attending appointments

- Negotiating offers and managing the sale
- Problem-solving
- Marketing

Because I gratefully have a team, I may delegate some of these roles, but as your transaction coordinator of all the details, nothing gets completed without my oversight and input into what needs to be done and how to get it done.

Of course, I have a workday, just like you, and because I have a well thought out systems-based business and for each client I draft a specific, strategic plan, most of my work is completed during normal business hours.

Responding

Theoretically, except for holidays, there are no official days off in real estate. I might have periods of times without any scheduled appointments, but there are *always* inquiries, emails and texts requiring a response. In our instant-response society, there really is little waiting until tomorrow. But, my clients come to trust me; my clients know that my team and I are working diligently towards their goals. Since part of our system includes a call or email every Tuesday, experience shows my clients rarely need to call or email me because they already know what is occurring.

When someone calls my office about a property, we respond. If other agents contact my office to ask questions about my clients listing or want to show one of our properties, we quickly get back to them. When an offer to purchase is received, and after I have reviewed and verified the information pertaining to the offer, I then contact my client to present it.

The workplace is anywhere I am and although I have my team in the office during normal business hours, on-call virtually on Saturday, it means I don't have to be in the office for the day to start — work happens at home, in the car, during vacations and on the go.

The job often begins early in the morning when I begin follow-up email communications, phone calls and texts about any number of things. You would find me sitting with my laptop and cell phone obtaining showing feedback on listings, following-up on in-progress transactions, updating clients on recent activity, answering questions and addressing any concerns, and creating to-do lists for myself and my assistants.

Scheduling Showings and Consultations

One of my team members will put together property itineraries for our homebuyer clients who are planning a house hunting trip. This usually involves numerous showings in a short period of time.

Scheduling these tours requires a delicate dance that takes into consideration geography and logistics against the backdrop of unknown time constraints that sellers may impose. ("Can you come at 2 p.m. instead of 10 a.m.?" or "Today's not good, but how about Friday?")

These impromptu changes in plan wouldn't be a problem if my buyer agents and I didn't have anything else to do. Some of our buyers have the luxury of time *and* they were local — but I'm rarely working with that kind of flexibility. And Murphy's Law says the property that's causing the scheduling difficulties will be the one at the top of our buyers' wish list. We always find a way to make it happen. But, while I'm sharing this, you as the home seller can consider how important it is to your success to be super flexible and willing to allow showings even at inconvenient times.

Setting and Attending Appointments

Then there are the appointments — meeting buyers and sellers for initial consultations, previewing and touring properties, meeting inspectors, meeting appraisers and a plethora of specialists, contractors, stagers, photographers and repair professionals.

While out on these meetings, business carries on and the emails, calls and texts flood in. Oftentimes my team and I will be juggling these meetings with the sellers from six months ago who call and want to meet immediately — or the buyer couple who suddenly found the perfect home that they need to see right away.

Negotiating Offers and Managing the Sale

The ever-important skill of negotiating offers may go on for days. Once an offer gets worked out and a property goes under contract, that is just the beginning of the next step. There's no jumping up and down, high-fiving and laughing all the way to the bank. Quite the contrary, this is where the next step of managing all the transactional details begins.

At this point, we have to make sure that everyone involved in this process does their job. From whatever side of the transaction they represent — buyer or seller — we need to make sure everyone is fulfilling their obligations of the transaction in a timely manner.

When a lender is involved, active and frequent communication is a *must* to ensure the loan process remains on track. We check in with the title company to verify the file is being handled and all details are being attended to. The team also address's anything unexpected that may arise and things always arise. But having an experienced real estate advisor, like me, will prove invaluable and make things as simple as possible…for you.

There are an endless number of tasks that must get done from contract to close, from reminding clients about utility transfers to ensuring the seller has everything moved out on the day so that we can hand over the keys to the buyer.

Problem-Solving

Problem-solving and crisis management happens at every turn. It includes educating my clients about the realities of what they are trying to accomplish, running down information about a community, association or property, and troubleshooting umpteen potential issues that could derail the transaction and ultimately the closing.

Unlike many jobs, one of the things that I love most is that no two days are the same. One week could be plagued by multiple snags (a buyer's financing falls apart, home inspection issues, etc.), and on another day, it all comes together in an eerily smooth manner. There is no guarantee that the time spent and the hours that my team and I put in will result in a paycheck.

I can't bill for the time and effort expended giving advice, giving accurate information, showing properties, attending inspections and appraisals, preparing for open house events and more. I work on a contingent basis and will only be reimbursed monetarily for all the team efforts when the home is sold. The other way I am compensated is when my outrageously happy client introduces me to their friends, family members, coworkers, you know, the people that they care about, who could use my help.

Marketing

Another part of the process is the marketing and business development. I pour my heart into my brand, my knowledge and my expertise. I have websites, newsletters, postcards, videos or other marketing pieces drawing attention to my sellers' homes and our ability to prepare, and sell homes. I devote thought and resources to each marketing piece with an eye toward implementation, execution and tracking results at every turn.

In short, real estate is a profession full of follow-up, follow-up, follow-up; multi-tasking, prioritizing, re-prioritizing; evaluating, advising and coaching, guiding, researching and problem-solving, and the ever-important communication.

Despite what reality television portrays, I don't simply ride around in an expensive car. I won't show up in designer clothes at some swanky place to negotiate a deal over trendy cocktails. It might appear glamorous and easy, but showing a customer properties or putting a home on the market happens sometime in the middle of a very involved process. Marketing, branding and creating top-of-mind presence usually comes first, and those are the things along with the proven results and introduction from happy clients that motivate customers to choose my team.

Real estate advisors, like me, are the catalyst for the *entire* process of preparing, marketing and successfully selling. And guiding clients from where they are to where they want to be is always at the forefront of what I do.

Raving Fans: What Past Clients Have to Share

Kim and her team were there for us when we needed to sell our Mom's home after she passed away. Kim and her staff were professional, courteous and prompt in resolving all issues involving the marketing and sales process of the home, and they were there through the whole Trust and Escrow process. I would highly recommend the Horizon Real Estate team to anyone that is faced with the overwhelming process of preparing, marketing and selling of a property that is involved in a Trust or Probate situation - **John K.**

We used Kim and her team to sell our house and I'm so glad we did! We had actually signed a contract with another agent who we were very disappointed with. Our house had been on the market for approximately five months with NO offers whatsoever! None! Then, one day when I was coming home from work, I saw a "For Sale" sign on the street behind ours. Always looking at our competition, I drove past the house. It didn't look much different from ours except it had a "SOLD" sign on it. I came home and told my husband about it. Well, we still had our house on the market a couple more weeks with no action and decided to go get the agents name so we could give her a call and see what she was about. Much to our horror, the sign was down and movers were there! I got out of the car and asked where the sign was and were the owners there so I could ask them. Luckily, the sign was on the side of the house, so I took a picture, went home and immediately called her. It was Kim Ward. I told her I needed someone aggressive and honest with our situation and house as far as why we weren't getting any offers. I cancelled our contract with the other agent, and met with Kim. She suggested that we do some "fine tuning" inside which really made a huge difference. Her team also came in and staged our house to the point where it looked so good we almost wanted to stay. It cost us a little bit, but when our house went on the market, we had one offer in three days and multiple offers by the end of the week. Kim and Laura were also very helpful in obtaining our new home. They didn't let anyone take advantage of us, and were so extremely knowledgeable. They really fought for us to get what we were looking for. There was never a time when we waited for questions to be answered or to go look at a house. They were so prompt and available to help us! Choosing the right agent is so completely important. I would so highly recommend this team in an instant! We not only had the best team, we made some great friends! Please give them a call, you will be so glad you did, just be ready to move! - **Frank and Carol K.**

We worked with Kim Ward and her team to facilitate a probate sale of my late brother's house. We live in the Phoenix area so it was complicated selling a house in San Diego. Kim and her team made a stressful job much, much easier. She was able to find us a handyman, a house cleaner, help us pick new carpeting and arrange for it to be installed, and recommend a good charity for us to donate unneeded furniture and household goods. We did not need to be present for anything except the furniture donation as we were keeping a few items. Her photographer took such beautiful photos for the listing that we received 5 offers, all above the listing price, within days of putting it on the market. We were delighted to be able to do almost this entire transaction long distance utilizing DocuSign for all signatures and, best of all, we received $26,000 over our asking price with the deal closing within 30 days. After working with Kim and her team, we wholeheartedly recommend them for any real estate transaction, especially a probate sale. We can't thank her enough! - **Steven and Lisa K.**

My wife is an attorney and her firm has used Kim's professional services for years. When it came time to list our condo in North Park she was the obvious choice. Kim did not simply assume she would get the business because of her existing business relationship with my wife, she provided us with a professional, comprehensive presentation explaining the entire process to us. Kim was a strong advocate in the negotiating process and offered her honest opinion when asked, which was refreshing and helpful. Kim sold our condo for about $20K more than we were expecting!!! I would highly recommend her to anyone looking to sell their home! We were also equally impressed with her colleague (and sister) Laura Massey as buyers as well; professionalism must run in the family!!! - **Eric and Chantelle W.**

My husband and I have worked with Kim Ward and her Horizon Real Estate team to both buy and sell a house. Buying our first house, Kim was very patient with us and explained each step of the way. This is so helpful for first-time home buyers! Selling our house was a good experience, too. She had good recommendations for staging our home to sell. She listened to any concerns we had while we were in escrow and addressed them immediately. Our sale was a bit unusual, and Kim fought to make it all go smoothly! You truly are in good hands with Kim Ward and her team. - **Drew and Carolyn C.**

Raving Fans: What Attorneys Have To Share

We are probate lawyers located in Los Angeles, and needed to sell an estate property in San Diego. We could not spend very much time in San Diego, so needed to hire a REALTOR® who understood the probate sale process in depth, and could take charge of the property clean-out, staging, and all the other details associated with the property and sale process. We interviewed several realtors and had to make a judgment quickly regarding who we felt we could trust with this project. We immediately felt very comfortable with Kim Ward. Her experience with probate sales, and her organization, is the best I have ever seen, and we work with realtors all the time. Her electronic update process is incredibly helpful; any time I thought of a question I needed to ask, I found it was answered before I asked. There were several challenging and sensitive elements to this particular property, and Kim and her team handled them with grace and professionalism.

We will certainly use her again the next time we have an estate property in the San Diego area. - **Anne Gifford, Esq.**

As a probate and real estate attorney, clients often request referrals for additional professionals, including real estate agents. I have recommended Kim Ward's services to many of my clients...and they have been thrilled with the results!

Typically probate administrators and trustees find themselves in the position of being an average person in the unusual situation of having to manage and liquidate the majority of assets of a deceased family member. Often such circumstances involve cleaning up and selling real property...in the midst of grieving the loss of a loved one. Kim's knowledge of estate administration circumstances, skill level in real estate marketing, and willingness to take on various additional related tasks (particularly for out of state administrators/trustees) have been a tremendous asset to many of my clients.

Kim has successfully and swiftly liquidated not only trust and estate single family homes, but the primary business property, condo and vacant lot as well. Kim remains a "go to" real estate professional for my office, and I gladly recommend her services to anyone who asked. - **Beth Atuatasi, Esq.**

Kim and her team at Horizon Real Estate are top-notch real estate professionals. Thanks to her, we recently closed escrow on our probate estate property at a near seven-figure selling price, and close to the listing price recommended by Kim. At every step along the way of the sales process, Kim's advice and recommendations were spot on. Because our property had considerable deferred maintenance, Kim recommended some improvements/repairs which upgraded the property in a cost-effective manner and enhanced its appeal to buyers. She has a very good eye for staging properties which we benefitted from in the sale of this property. And when we got several offers at the same time, she suggested a multiple counter-offer. We took her advice and one party -- the eventual buyer -- accepted our counter-offer. There were some further negotiations on repairs after the buyer commissioned an inspection of the property and Kim's negotiating skills were again put to good use on our behalf. This was a unique property in many respects and there were many issues to be dealt with in closing the sale but Kim and her team handled everything with great attention to detail. Her follow-through and responsiveness were outstanding. I have absolutely no hesitation in highly recommending Kim and her team. She was a pleasure to work with from start to finish and her representation of our interests was superlative. You cannot go wrong by choosing Kim and her team at Horizon Real Estate to handle the sale of your real property. **- Frank Walker, Esq.**

ABOUT THE AUTHOR

Kim Ward has been actively involved with real estate for over two decades. As far back as 1989, Kim and her husband, Dave, began purchasing and renovating residential property. They did this while working full time and raising four children. From these experiences, Kim learned valuable critical thinking skills, successful multi-tasking, and how to nurture relationships. Their children have grown into independent, well-adjusted young adults, so those skills seem to have paid off.

Her first estate representative client was introduced by his attorney in 2003. Kim's skilled and dedicated team has now helped over 400 estate representatives' through the process of preparing, marketing, and successfully selling homes in San Diego county. Because of those experiences, Kim and her team have become the authority to help estate representatives through the complicated job of being responsible for someone's estate.

Kim's life philosophy influences everything she does. It's the "can do" approach to any challenge, coupled with her positive attitude, that contributes to building a successful real estate business. Kim says, "When you really love what you do, it doesn't feel like work. The trust that comes from working with our clients makes the help my team and I provide the most rewarding part of my job."

Kim Ward's Memberships

CRS-Certified Residential Specialist

SDCBA-Affiliate Member San Diego County Bar Association

PFAC-Affiliate Member of Professional Fiduciary Association of California

CPREA -Certified Probate Real Estate Advisor

Member of San Diego, California and National Association of REALTORS®

Member of By Referral Only and BroVance

Member of San Diego Women's Foundation

Made in the USA
Columbia, SC
07 April 2019